23 22 21 20 19 18 17 16 1 2 3 4 5 6 7 8

ISBN: 978-1506408828

Library of Congress Cataloging-in-Publication Data

Names: Grosche, Erwin, 1955- author. | Teich, Karsten, 1967- illustrator.
Title: Jonah and the whale / Erwin Grosche, Karsten Teich.
Other titles: Jona und der Wal. English
Description: Minneapolis : Sparkhouse Family, 2016.
Identifiers: LCCN 2015046647 | ISBN 9781506408828 (hardcover : alk. paper)
Subjects: LCSH: Jonah (Biblical prophet)--Juvenile literature. | Bible
    stories, English--Jonah.
Classification: LCC BS580.J55 G7613 2016 | DDC 224/.9209505--dc23
LC record available at http://lccn.loc.gov/2015046647

Printed in China

9781506408828; VN0003466; APR2016

Erwin Grosche

Jonah and the Whale

Karsten Teich

Sparkhouse Family

MINNEAPOLIS

"Just what I needed," Jonah groaned,
stretching and yawning wide as the sky.
He had been dozing in the warm sun,
when God woke him up.

God said to Jonah, "Go to Nineveh,
the great city, and proclaim this message:
God is going to destroy Nineveh,
because the people there are evil."

"Just what I needed!" Jonah scowled.
He didn't want this job.
He decided to run away from God.

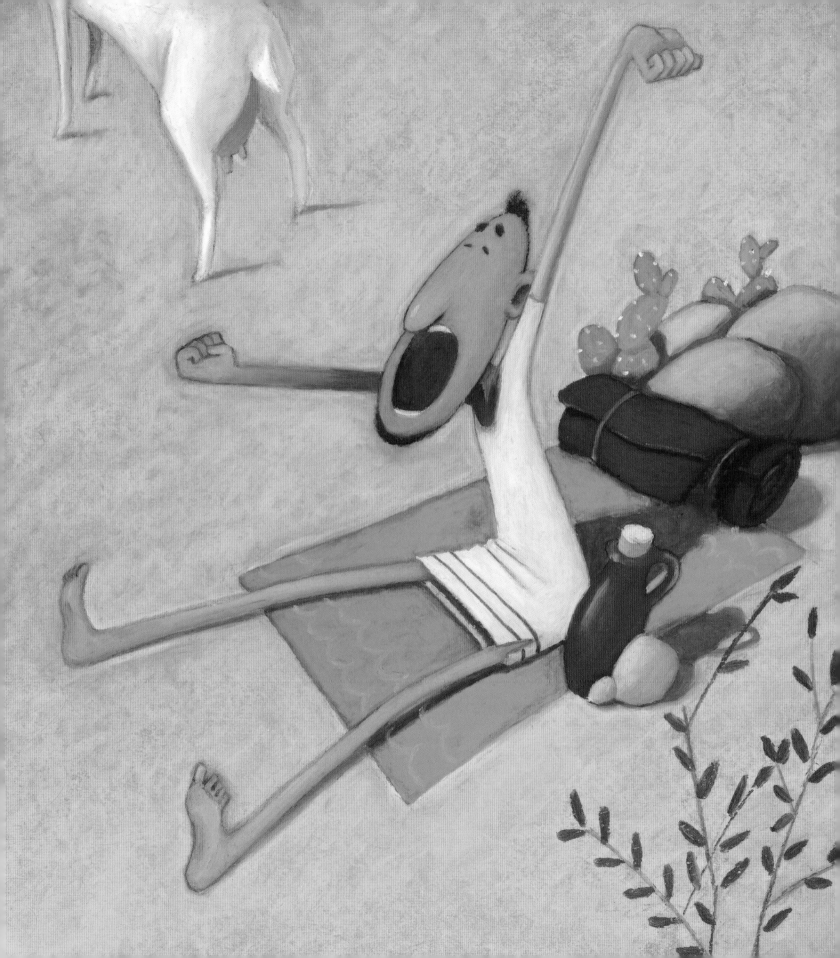

Jonah ran to the harbor and found a ship whose captain would take him aboard. He wanted to get as far away from God as possible. Jonah hid below deck with the ship's cargo and fell fast asleep. His voyage at sea began.

Suddenly, God threw a mighty wind upon the sea.

A great storm rose up, bashing the ship with its raging waves.

The terrified sailors cried out for help, but their gods did not respond.

To make the ship lighter, they threw everything they could overboard.

But the ship still threatened to sink. And Jonah continued to sleep.

The captain rushed below deck to wake Jonah.
"A storm is raging! It's trying to pull our ship to the bottom of the sea!
How can you sleep?"
"Just what I needed," Jonah groaned. He admitted to the captain that
he was running away from God's call.
"It's *your* fault?" the captain cried in despair. "What shall we do?"

Jonah blinked blearily at the captain. "The last thing I need is for
something to happen to you and your sailors. Throw me into the sea.
The storm will stop, and you can continue on your journey."

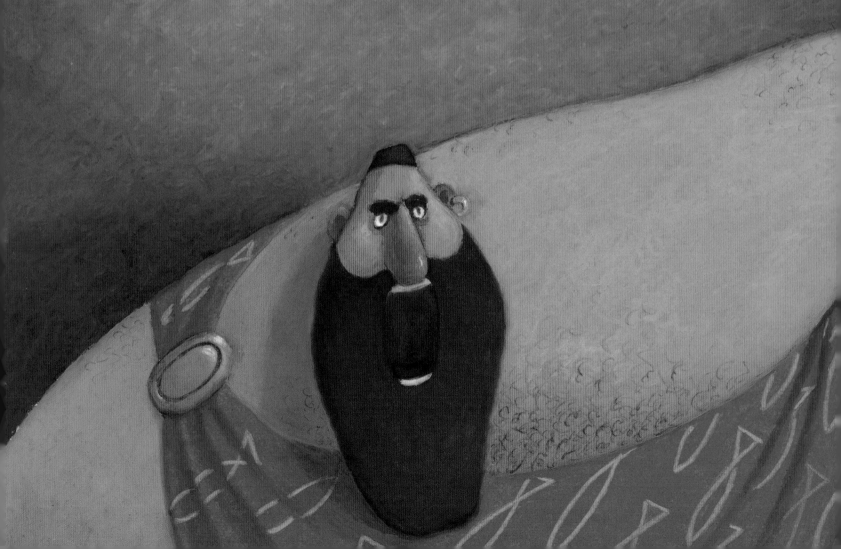

The captain shook his head. "Use all your strength to row to shore!"
he shouted at his men. But the waves crashed
higherand higher, spilling onto the deck.
The wind howled with rage, and the crew howled back in fear.
Finally, the captain gave in. The crew threw Jonah into the sea.
At once, the storm stopped.
The sea ceased its raging.

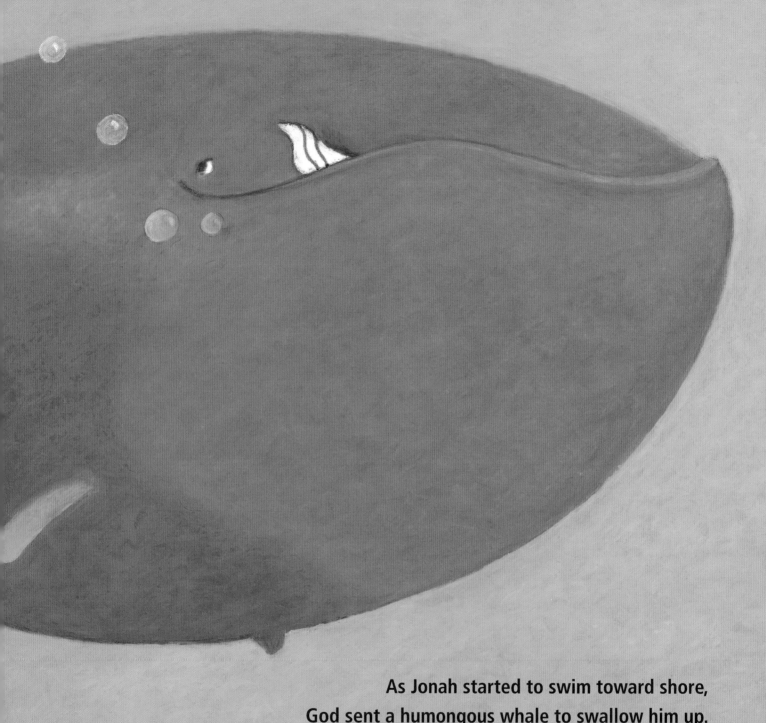

As Jonah started to swim toward shore,
God sent a humongous whale to swallow him up.
With a slurp, Jonah slid into the belly of the enormous creature.
He looked around, terrified. When he realized he was okay,
Jonah once again lay down to sleep. But the fish jostled
him back and forth so much that Jonah could not rest.

"Just what I needed!" Jonah cried out to God. "Why can't you leave me alone?
First you hurl me into the sea and now this?" Jonah was miserable.

Jonah spent three long days and three long nights
inside the belly of the fish praying to God.

"Okay, I give up. I'll go to Nineveh and deliver your message to the people,"
Jonah said reluctantly. So God commanded the fish to spit Jonah onto the shore.
Jonah let the warm sun dry his clothes and then left for Nineveh.

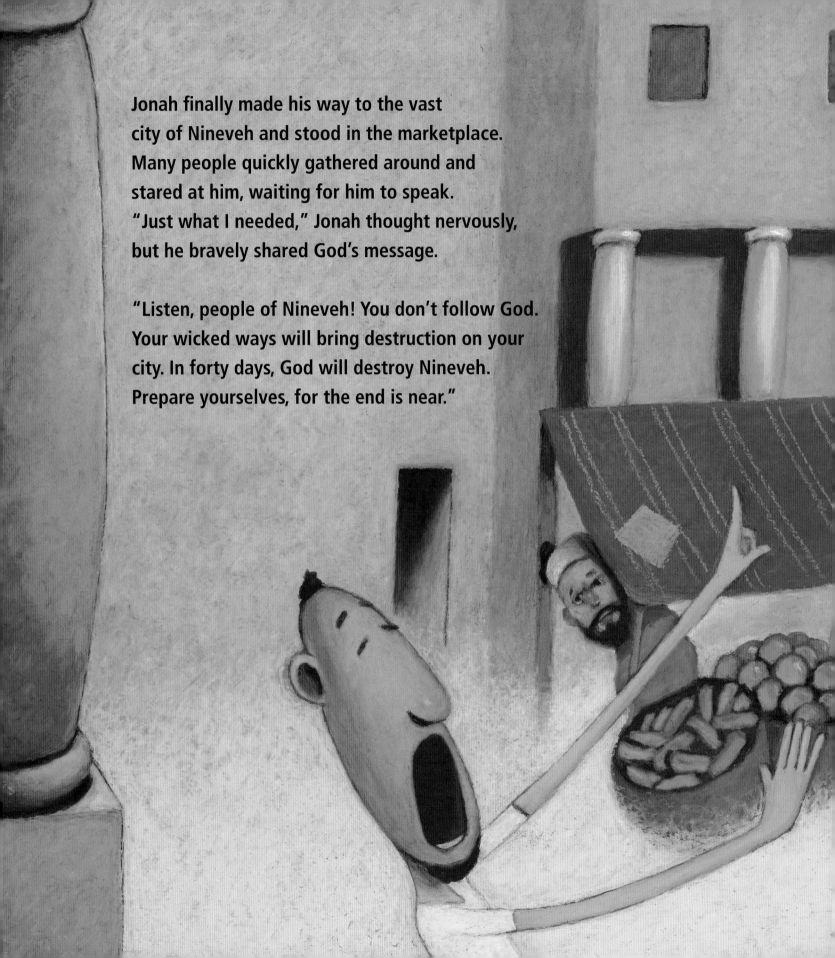

Jonah finally made his way to the vast
city of Nineveh and stood in the marketplace.
Many people quickly gathered around and
stared at him, waiting for him to speak.
"Just what I needed," Jonah thought nervously,
but he bravely shared God's message.

"Listen, people of Nineveh! You don't follow God.
Your wicked ways will bring destruction on your
city. In forty days, God will destroy Nineveh.
Prepare yourselves, for the end is near."

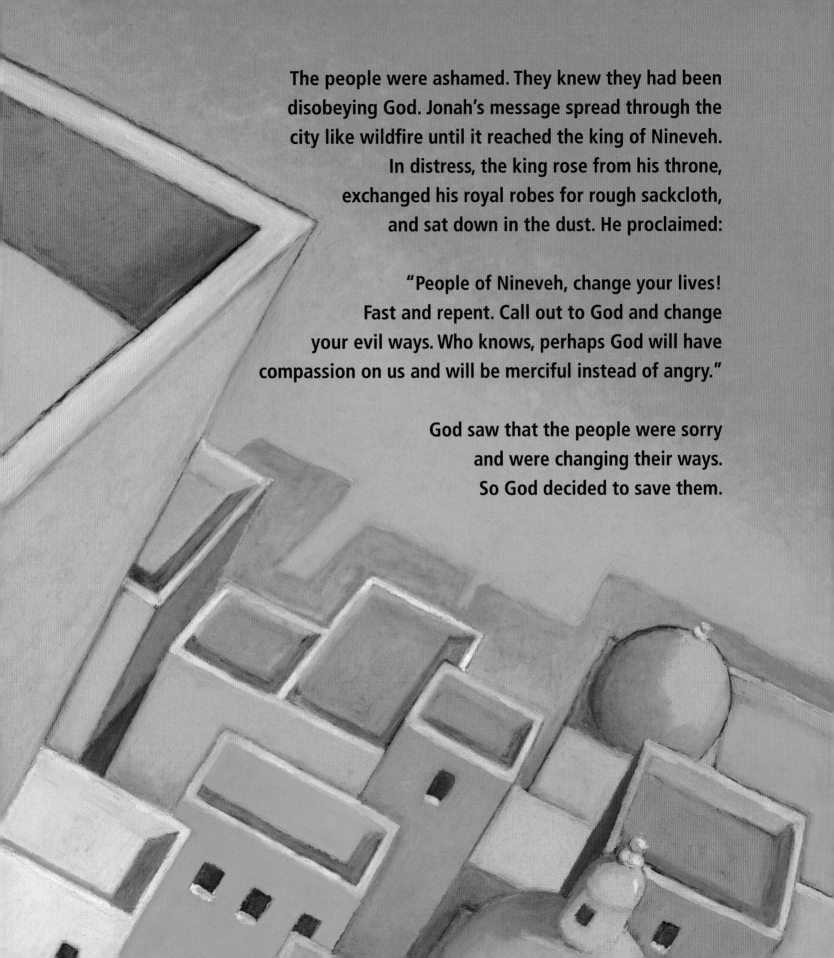

The people were ashamed. They knew they had been
disobeying God. Jonah's message spread through the
city like wildfire until it reached the king of Nineveh.
In distress, the king rose from his throne,
exchanged his royal robes for rough sackcloth,
and sat down in the dust. He proclaimed:

"People of Nineveh, change your lives!
Fast and repent. Call out to God and change
your evil ways. Who knows, perhaps God will have
compassion on us and will be merciful instead of angry."

God saw that the people were sorry
and were changing their ways.
So God decided to save them.

Unhappy and annoyed, Jonah left the city and called out to God.
"I have always known you are a gracious and compassionate God.
Your kindness is so great that you forgive when people repent with their hearts.
But what was the point of making me come here if you weren't going
to destroy the city like you said? You woke me up, sent me off,
and left me alone with your words," Jonah fumed.
Jonah was so angry and disappointed that he paced back and forth
until he ran out of energy. He sat and watched the city
to see what would happen until he fell asleep.

God decided to teach Jonah a lesson so that he could learn what love is.

As Jonah awoke the next morning, he was surprised to see
a bush growing above him, providing a cooling shade.
"Just what I needed," Jonah rejoiced.
He sat under the bush all day and thanked God.
But the next night, God sent a worm to eat the roots
of the bush until it withered and dried up.

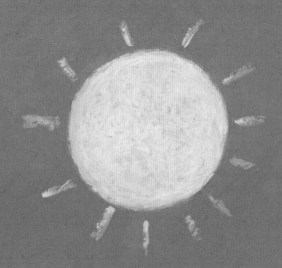

"Just what I needed," Jonah pouted. "I can't believe my shady bush is dead.
I have nothing to protect me now from the sun and wind."

God laughed. "Jonah, you are just what I needed when I asked you to
proclaim my message to the people of Nineveh. But you ran away instead.
Now you are so concerned about this bush that you neither planted nor watered.
Can't you understand how much I must care for the people of Nineveh, who
I created? I love all my children, even those who try to run away from me."

Jonah thought back to the storm and the big fish and the shady bush.
God had done all of this to show how much Jonah was loved.
Jonah looked to God and no longer needed anything.

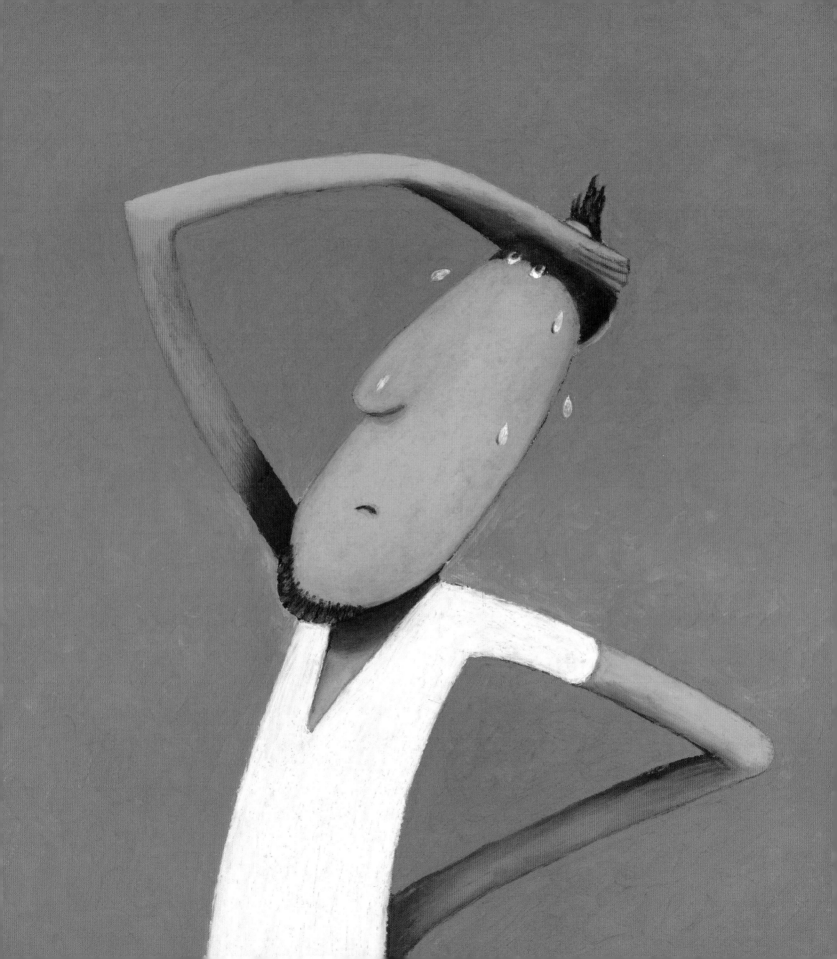